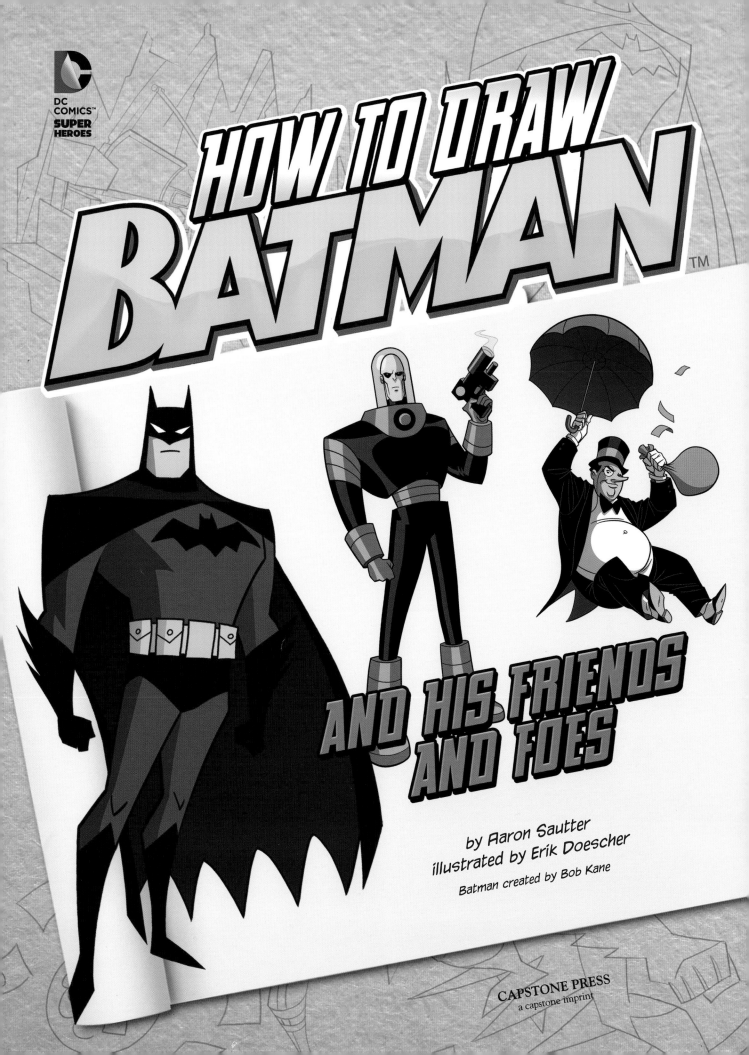

DC COMICS™ SUPER HEROES

HOW TO DRAW BATMAN™

AND HIS FRIENDS AND FOES

by Aaron Sautter
illustrated by Erik Doescher
Batman created by Bob Kane

CAPSTONE PRESS
a capstone imprint

Published in 2015 by Capstone Press,
a Capstone Imprint
1710 Roe Crest Drive
North Mankato, Minnesota 56003
www.capstonepub.com

Library of Congress Cataloging-in-Publication Data
Sautter, Aaron.
How to draw Batman and his friends and foes / by Aaron Sautter, illustrated by Erik Doescher.
pages cm.–(DC super heroes. Drawing DC super heroes)
Summary: "Simple, step-by-step instructions teach readers how to draw Batman and
his friends and enemies"–Provided by publisher.
ISBN 978-1-4914-2153-6 (library binding)
1. Cartoon characters–Juvenile literature. 2. Batman (Fictitious character)–Juvenile literature.
3. Drawing–Technique–Juvenile literature. I. Doescher, Erik. II. Title.
NC1764.8.H47S278 2015
741.5'1–dc23   2014023861

Credits
Designer: Ted Williams
Art Director: Nathan Gassman
Production Specialist: Kathy McColley

Design Elements
Capstone Studio: Karon Dubke; Shutterstock: Artishok, Bennyartist, Eliks, gst, Mazzzur, Roobcio

Printed in the United States of America in North Mankato, Minnesota.
092014   008482CGS15

DRAWING PROJECTS

LET'S DRAW THE DARK KNIGHT!

He's been called the World's Greatest Detective, the Caped Crusader, and the Dark Knight. But whatever people choose to call him—Batman is a criminal's worst nightmare.

As a young boy, Bruce Wayne lost his parents, Thomas and Martha, during a robbery in a dark alley. Bruce took his parents' death very hard. He swore an oath that he would do whatever it took to rid Gotham City of criminals and crime. To achieve his goal, Bruce studied criminology to learn detective skills. He also trained hard to become an expert in martial arts. He even became a master of disguise and an expert escape artist.

Bruce's new skills were useful, but they weren't enough for him. He also wanted to strike fear into the hearts of lawbreakers. Bruce chose to use his own fear of bats as inspiration. He made a special suit resembling a giant bat to hide his identity and to frighten hardened criminals. With his Batsuit and unmatched crime-fighting skills, Bruce became Batman, the Dark Knight!

Welcome to the world of Batman! On the following pages you'll learn to draw Batman, his friends, and several of his most infamous enemies.

Imagine the streets of Gotham City and see what kind of amazing Batman drawings you can create!

WHAT YOU'LL NEED

You don't need superpowers to draw mighty heroes. But you'll need some basic tools. Gather the following supplies before starting your awesome art.

PAPER: You can get special drawing paper from art supply and hobby stores. But any type of blank, unlined paper will work fine.

PENCILS: Drawings should always be done in pencil first. Even the pros use them. If you make a mistake, it'll be easy to erase and redo it. Keep plenty of these essential drawing tools on hand.

PENCIL SHARPENER: To make clean lines, you need to keep your pencils sharp. Get a good pencil sharpener. You'll use it a lot.

ERASERS: As you draw, you're sure to make mistakes. Erasers give artists the power to turn back time and erase those mistakes. Get some high quality rubber or kneaded erasers. They'll last a lot longer than pencil erasers.

BLACK MARKER PENS: When your drawing is ready, trace over the final lines with black marker pen. The dark lines will help make your characters stand out on the page.

COLORED PENCILS AND MARKERS: Ready to finish your masterpiece? Bring your characters to life and give them some color with colored pencils or markers.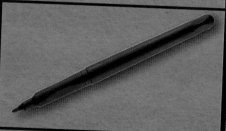

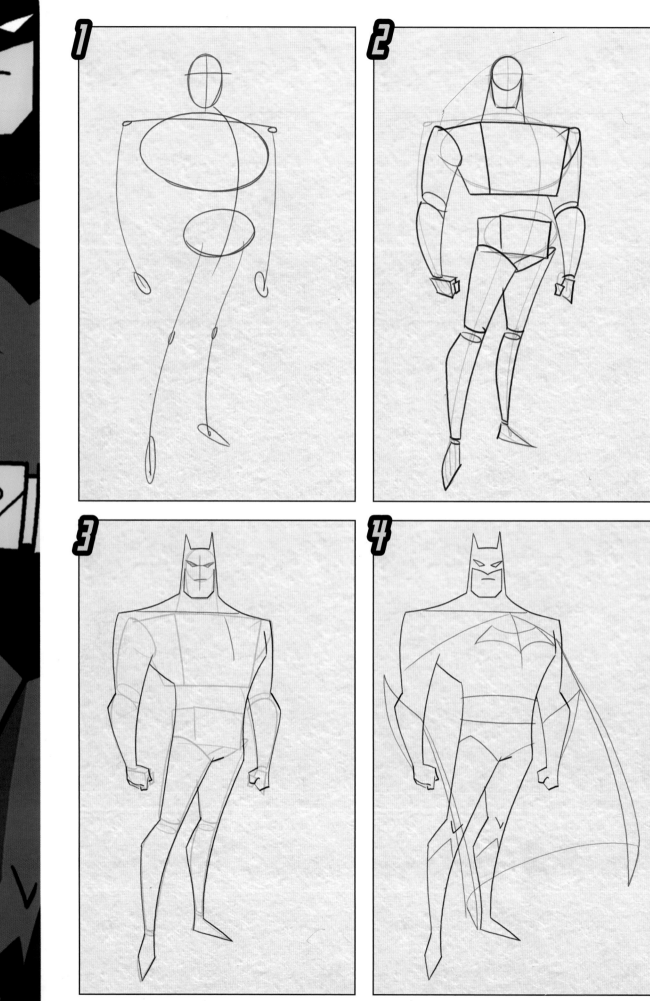

1

2

3

4

BATSUIT

Batman wouldn't be Batman without his Batsuit. The suit's main purpose is to hide Bruce Wayne's identity while striking terror in the hearts of criminals. The suit also helps Batman hide in the shadows as he prowls through the night. Batman's utility belt holds his many crime-fighting tools, including batarangs, a grapnel, binoculars, and remote controls for his vehicles.

5

BATCAVE

Sometimes the World's Greatest Detective needs a quiet place to think. When Batman needs answers, he heads to his secret Batcave. There he uses the powerful Batcomputer to study clues and learn the information he needs. The Batcave is also home to Batman's amazing vehicles and his workshop where he creates his incredible crime-fighting gadgets.

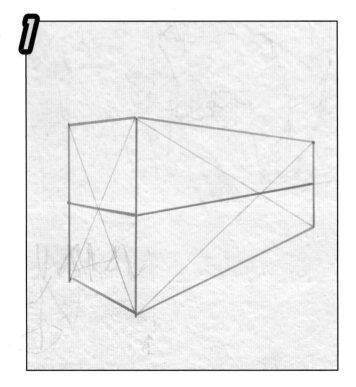

1

DRAWING IDEA
Next try drawing the Batmobile blasting
out of the Batcave's secret entrance!

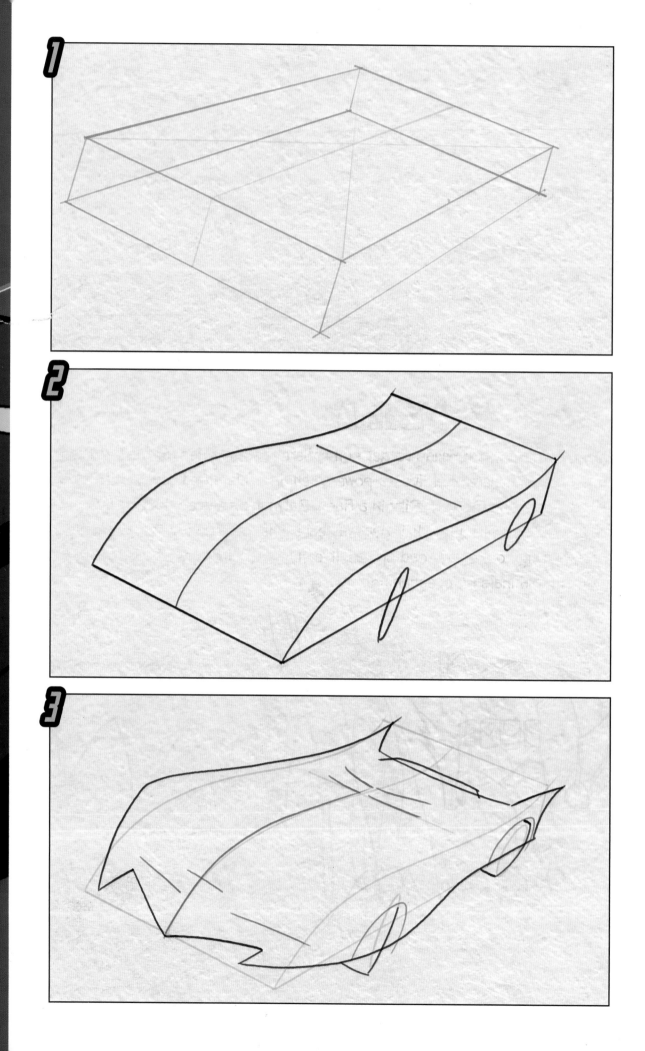

BATMOBILE

When Batman needs to get somewhere fast, he relies on the Batmobile to get him there. With its jet-powered engine, this speedy car helps Batman travel across Gotham City in a flash. Batman also uses the Batmobile to chase down villains in their getaway cars. The armored car is equipped with grappling hooks and road spikes. It can also create slippery oil slicks to stop criminals from escaping.

DRAWING IDEA
Try drawing the Batmobile chasing Two-Face's getaway car after a bank robbery!

FIGHTING CRIME

Criminals in Gotham City don't stand a chance with Batman around. He's always on the lookout for thugs trying to break the law. When a super-villain like Bane tries to rob a bank, the Dark Knight is on the case. Bane is very intelligent and has superhuman strength. But Batman's fighting skills and experience can stop the master criminal in his tracks!

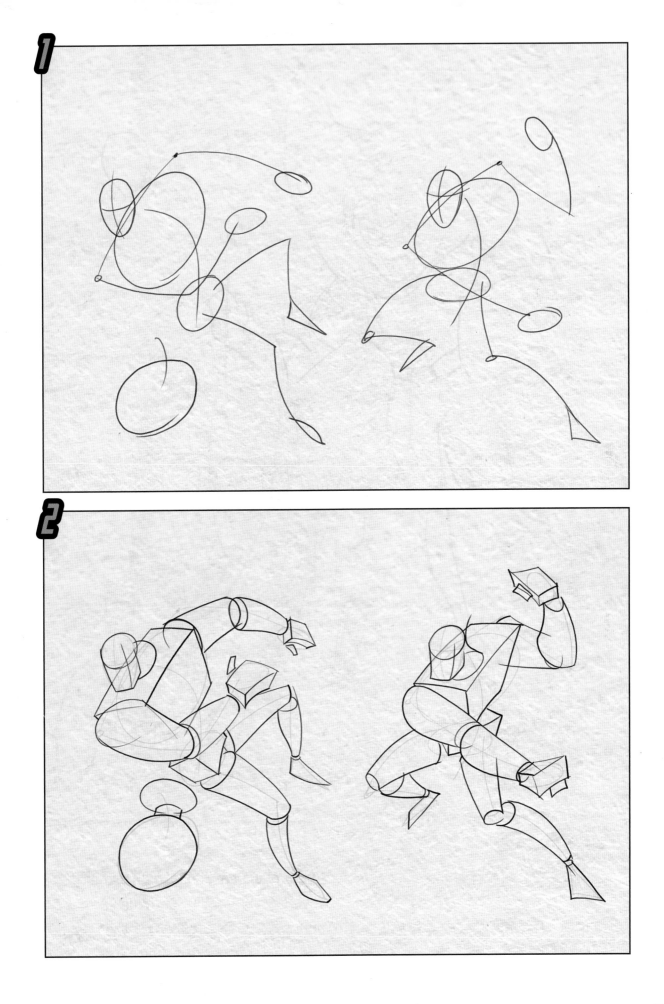

DRAWING IDEA
After drawing Robin, try drawing him fighting next to Batman to put a stop to the Riddler's plans!

ROBIN, THE BOY WONDER

Real Name: Tim Drake

Home Base: Gotham City

Occupation: student, crime fighter

Abilities: martial arts expert, investigation skills

Background: Tim Drake is quite brilliant for his age. Using his keen observation skills, Tim learned the secret identities of both Batman and Nightwing. Nightwing had once fought crime next to Batman as the first Robin. Nightwing then helped Tim convince Batman that he needed a new partner. Tim now fights crime alongside Batman as the all new Robin, the Boy Wonder.

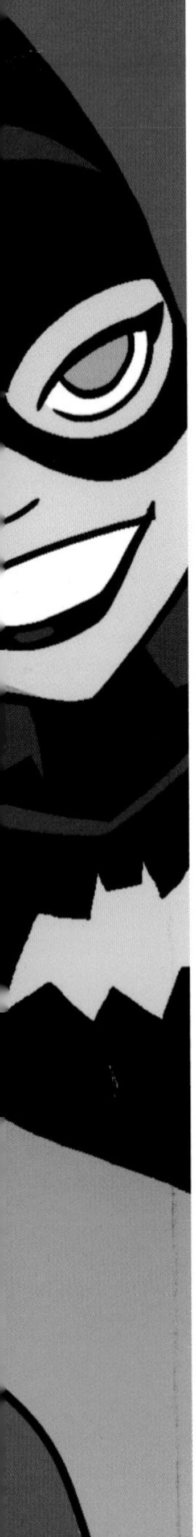

1

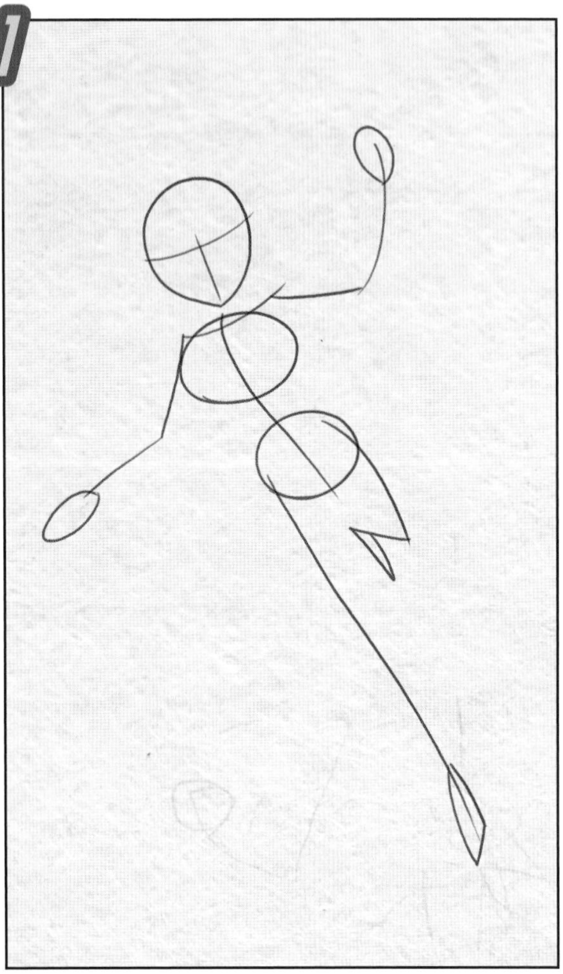

2

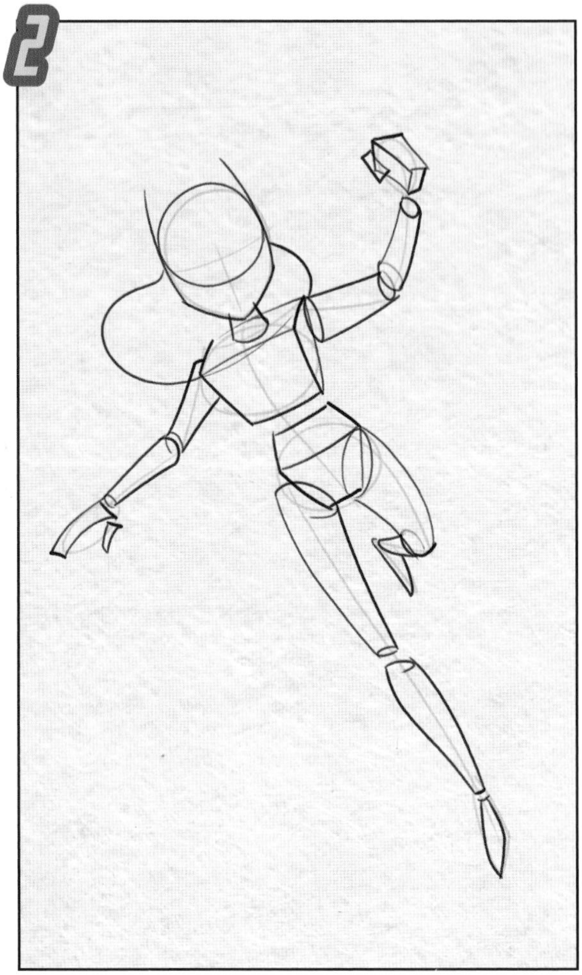

3

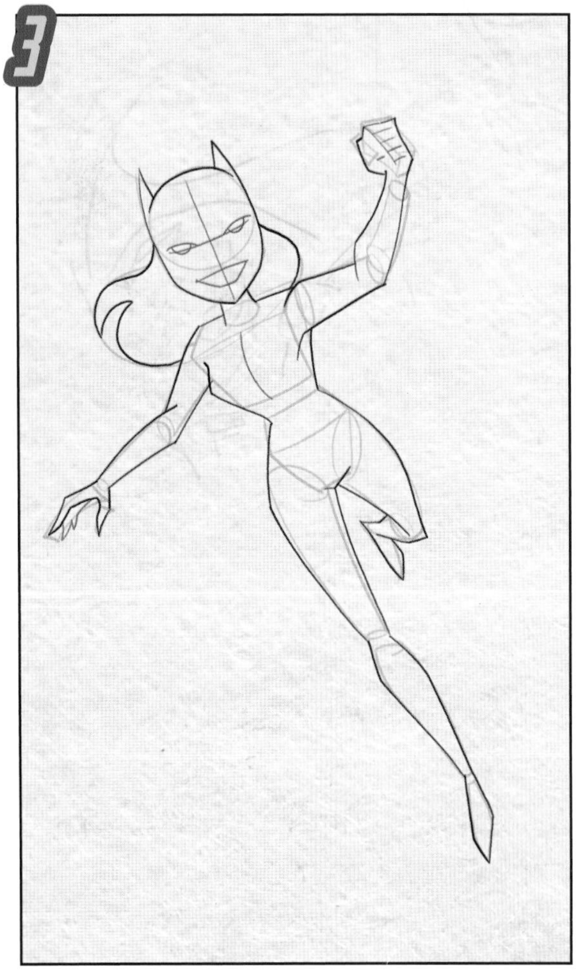

4

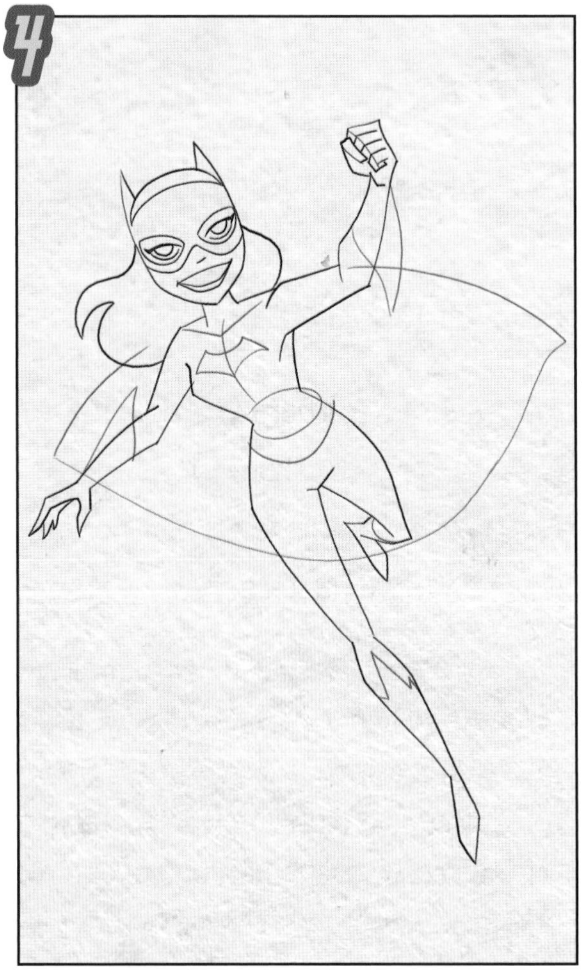

BATGIRL

Real Name: Barbara Gordon

Home Base: Gotham City

Occupation: college student, crime fighter

Abilities: gymnastics, martial arts skills

Background: Barbara Gordon takes after her father, Police
Commissioner James Gordon. She is strong-willed and dedicated to
wiping out crime in Gotham City. When Barbara's father was framed
for a crime he didn't commit, she made her own bat-themed suit and
attempted to break him out of jail. Since then Batgirl has become part
of Batman's team, helping him defend Gotham City from crime.

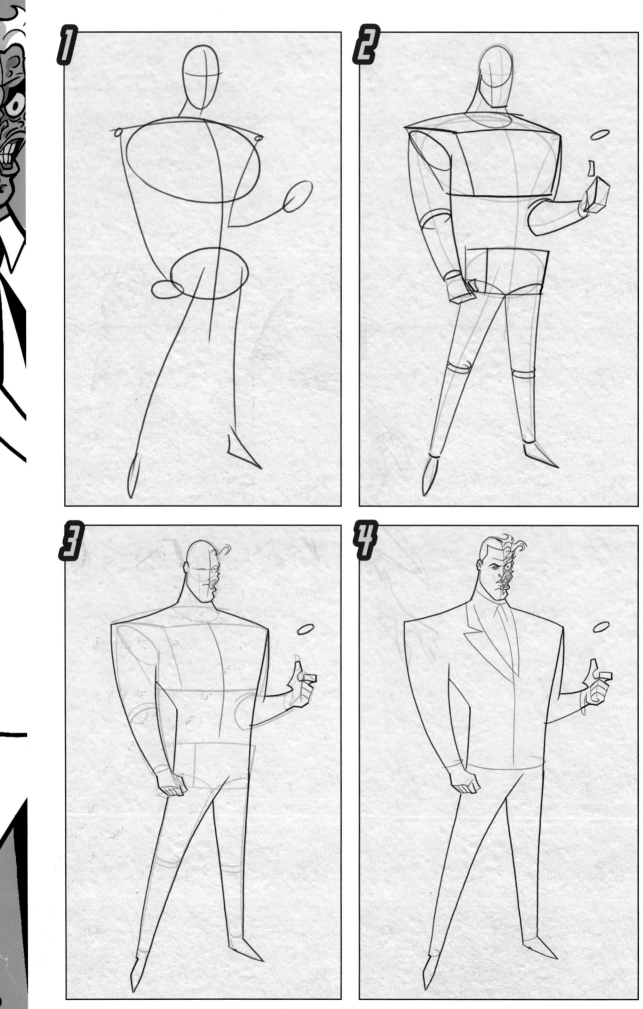

TWO-FACE

Real Name: Harvey Dent
Home Base: Gotham City
Occupation: professional criminal
Enemy of: Batman
Abilities: above-average strength and fighting skills, expert marksmanship
Equipment: special two-headed coin to make most decisions

Background: Harvey Dent was once the best prosecuting attorney in Gotham City. He worked tirelessly to send the city's most dangerous criminals to jail. But when an explosion scarred half of his face and body, Harvey's darker side took control. He became the criminal Two-Face. Now he tries to run the same criminal world he once fought so hard to bring to justice.

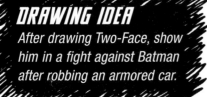

DRAWING IDEA
After drawing Two-Face, show him in a fight against Batman after robbing an armored car.

THE PENGUIN

Real Name: Oswald Cobblepot

Home Base: Gotham City

Occupation: professional criminal

Enemy of: Batman

Abilities: genius intelligence, numerous criminal connections

Equipment: trick umbrellas

Background: Oswald Cobblepot's waddling walk and beakish nose earned him the nickname of the Penguin. He is almost always protected by several hired thugs. The Penguin also owns a number of special umbrellas that hide a variety of deadly weapons. Among these are a machine gun, a flamethrower, a sword, small blades, and poison gas.

1

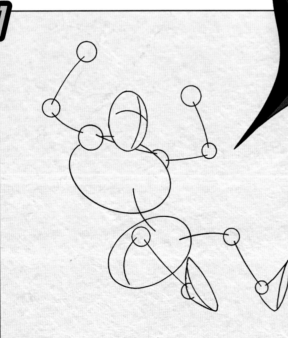

DRAWING IDEA
Next try drawing the Penguin trying to escape from Batman using his special umbrellas!

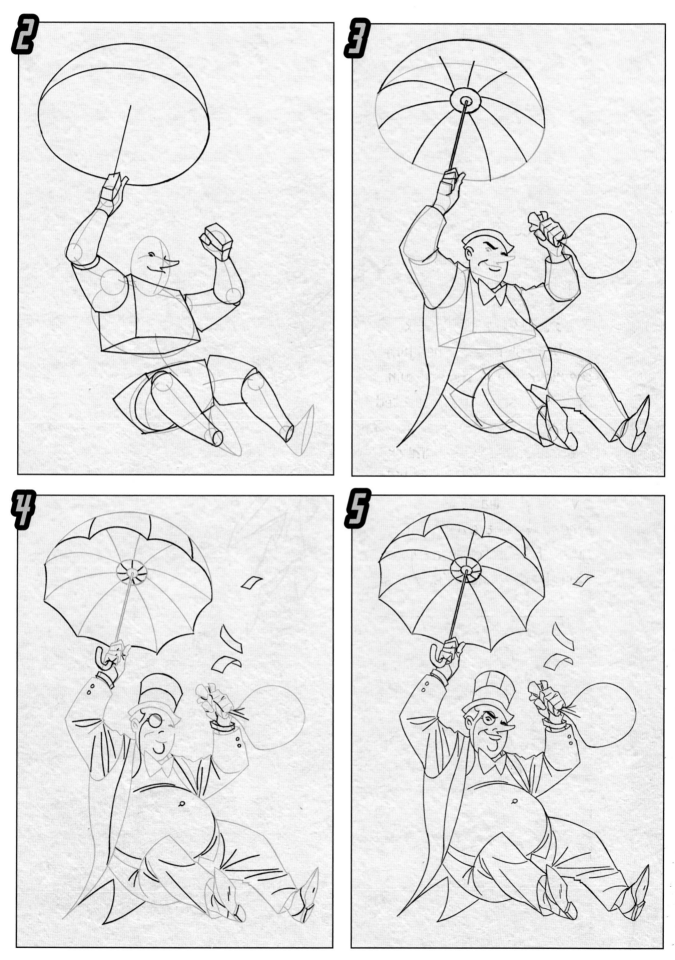

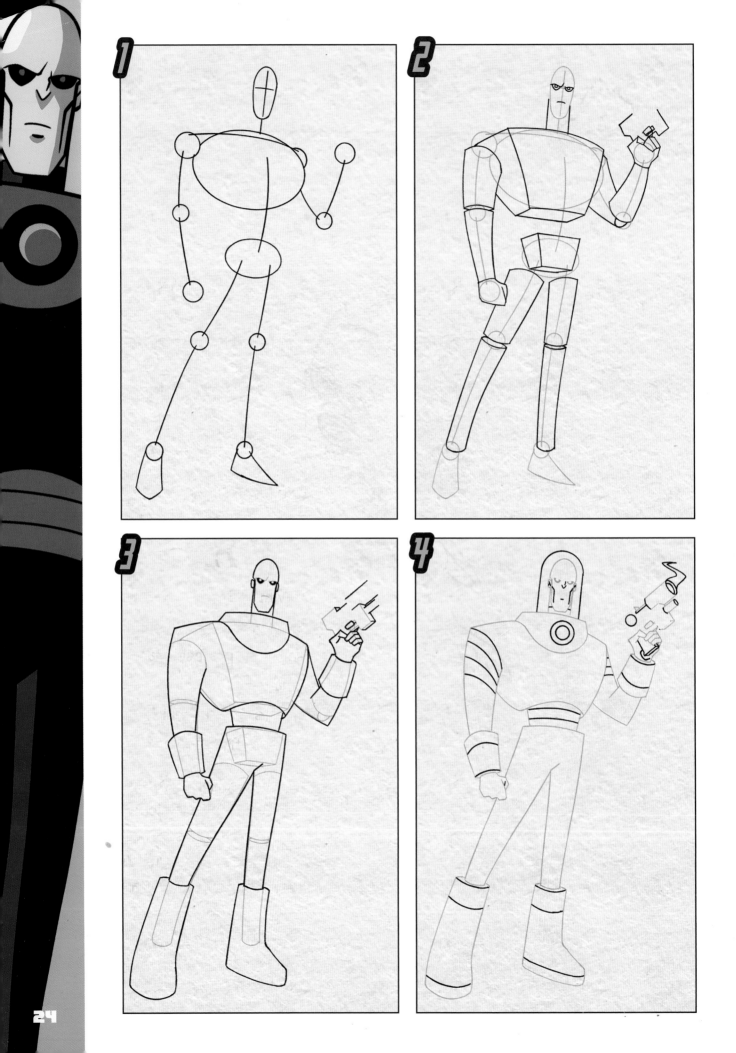

DRAWING IDEA
Try drawing Mr. Freeze stopping Batman in his tracks with his freeze gun!

5

MR. FREEZE

Real Name: Dr. Victor Fries

Home Base: Gotham City

Occupation: scientist, professional criminal

Enemy of: Batman

Abilities: enhanced strength, genius intellect

Equipment: cryo-suit, freeze gun

Background: One day scientist Victor Fries was accidentally soaked with chemicals in his lab. The accident changed his body so he could live only at sub-zero temperatures. To survive Victor built a special suit that keeps his body cold and gives him superhuman strength. To get the diamonds needed to power his suit, Victor turned to a life of crime. Calling himself Mr. Freeze, he uses a special freeze gun to aid him in his criminal activities.

1

THE RIDDLER

Real Name: Edward Nygma

Home Base: Gotham City

Occupation: professional criminal

Enemy of: Batman

Abilities: genius-level intellect

Equipment: question mark cane containing hidden weapons and gadgets

Background: Edward Nygma loved riddles and puzzles as a boy. When he grew up he invented a popular video game called *Riddle of the Minotaur*. The game sold millions of copies, but Nygma never got a penny for his work. To get his revenge, he became the genius criminal the Riddler. He enjoys leaving cryptic clues to his crimes. Only Batman can solve the Riddler's puzzling crimes and put a stop to his wicked plans.

DRAWING IDEA
Next try showing the Riddler using his special cane to try to outwit Batman during a fight!

STOPPING THE JOKER

The Joker loves being Batman's archenemy. He's always hoping to get the last laugh on the Dark Knight. The Joker enjoys designing weapons with a comical look to hide their true danger. For example, a huge bomb filled with deadly Joker Venom might look like a big party toy. But Batman is very familiar with how the Clown Prince of Crime thinks. He's always ready to swing into action and put a stop to the Joker's plans before innocent people get hurt.

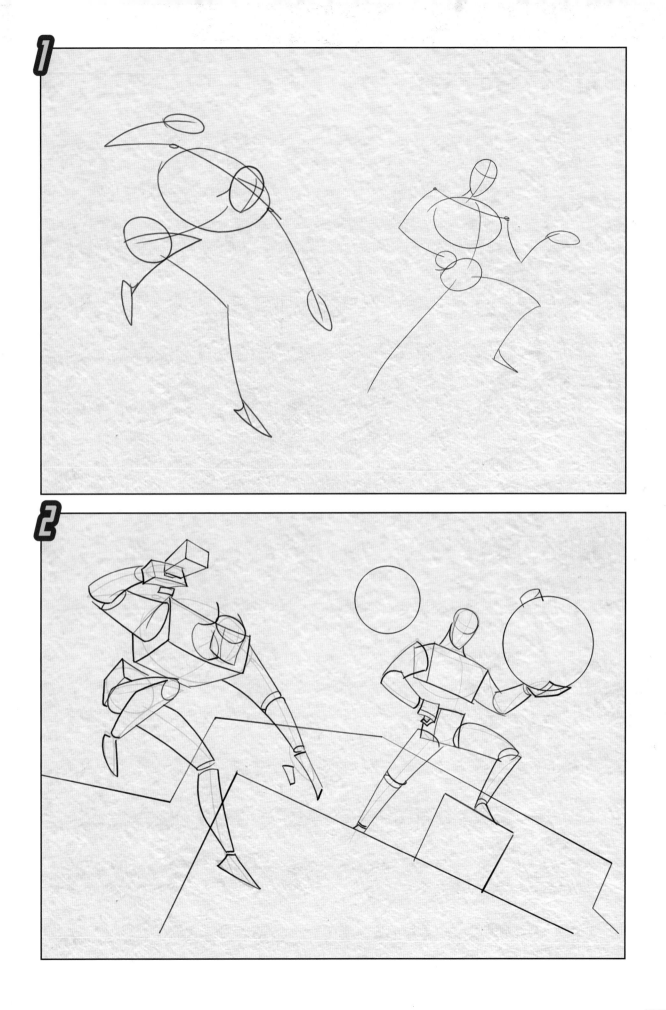

INTERNET SITES

FactHound offers a safe, fun way to find Internet sites related to this book.
All of the sites on FactHound have been researched by our staff.

Here's all you do:

Visit *www.facthound.com*

Type in this code: 9781491421536

TITLES IN THIS SET